HIP HOP ENGLISH

compiled by Michael Janes

ABSON BOOKS LONDON 5 Sidney Square London E1 2EY
Tel 020 7790 4737 Fax 020 7790 7346
email absonbooks@aol.com

Abson Books London
First published March 2003
Third impression April 2004
Cover design Chris Bird

Printed by Gutenberg Press, Malta
ISBN 0 902920 93 6

PREFACE

Hip hop originated back in the seventies in the Bronx, New York City, during the disco era. Black DJs like Kool Herc or Afrika Bambaataa began singing over the instrumental sections of the popular music of the time such as reggae. These black 'poets' or 'storytellers' set their words to a simple beat, and their musical style, which later developed into rap, made it possible for young black New Yorkers to express themselves freely and with imagination. Rap music has since become hugely popular, creating with it a totally new kind of spoken language and lifestyle: hip hop.

Modern street slang is made up chiefly of the language of hip hop and is spoken by young people around the world as they listen to rap music in ever-increasing numbers. TV programmes such as 'Da Ali G Show' have done a lot to raise people's awareness of the language.

Sure, lots of rap songs contain violent or crude language and drug terms, words like *bag up, pootie-tang* or *zooted*, often reflecting the roughness of ghetto life. However, many songs are created as a protest against or as an escape from these harsh everyday realities, while many others show the gentler or more positive side of hip hop – reflected in words and expressions such as *wordsmith, drop science, dime* or *bodacious*. We find lots of words too underlying the central importance of music in the hip hop lifestyle, words like *banger, b-boy, bo selecta, cipher* or *grip*. And there are a number of words referring to fashion: many rappers are smart dressers *g'd up* with their *bling bling*.

From its origins as an artistic form of self-expression for young black urban New Yorkers, hip hop has come a long way, for example, in the UK mixing with British and West Indian slang. Hip hop has developed into a language used by people everywhere when they want to be cool, or when they want to assert their own values against the values of the older generation.

A special thanks to my kids, Daniel and Leah, for all their hard work. Without them this book would not have taken off. Many thanks also to Rick Thorne, music journalist, for his insightful suggestions on reading the manuscript.

Michael Janes

A

a	going to, e.g. *I'm a do this*
ace	friend
aight (rhymes with right)	all right (often used in questions, e.g. *Aight?*)
all gravy	good, fine
all that	having lots of good qualities, e.g. *My boo's all that*
am (rhymes with Pam)	morning, e.g. *getting up in the am*
(from) around the way	from the neighbourhood
ass out	mess up, misbehave
Audi 5000	out of here, leaving, e.g. *I'm Audi 5000* (comes from the name of the car – it got recalled and not many were seen)
axe	ask

aye	yes	
ayo!	hello!	
ay yo trip!	hey (used to get attention)	

back in the day	a long time ago	
bad	good	
bag up	(a) arrest, jail	
	(b) laugh uncontrollably	
	(c) have sex with	
	(d) kill	
baller	(a) sportsperson, basketball player	
	(b) big-time wealthy hustler	
banger	(a) rock fan (short for headbanger)	
	(b) good song	

banging	exciting
battle	(a) compete with, e.g. *I'm battling him in a cipher*
	(b) competition
batty	(a) buttocks
	(b) ridiculous
	(c) homosexual, e.g. *Are you batty?*
batty boy	homosexual
b-boy, b-girl	(a) breakdancer (breakdancing is fast solo dancing and body spinning)
	(b) someone well into hip hop culture
bean	head, brain
bend	prostitute
Benjamins	hundred-dollar bills (American term, from Benjamin Franklin – his face appears on the 100-dollar bill)

bent	(a) sad
	(b) drunk
	(c) stoned
big dog	person in charge
big face money	US bills of large amounts
big up	(a) well done, e.g. *Big up to you!*
	(b) used for introducing a performer
big it up	applaud, e.g. *Big it up for da crew!*
bird	(a) kilo
	(b) female
biscuit	gun
biscuits	buttocks
bitching	excellent
bite	steal

bizzo	(a) bizarre individual
	(b) female, often someone's girlfriend
blast	play music loud
bling bling	(a) jewellery (especially showy gold or diamond rings and pendants)
	(b) showy
	(c) wearing showy jewellery
	(comes from the sparkle on jewellery reflecting the light. From the B.G. 1999 record called 'Bling Bling')
bo	good
bodacious	cool, great
bomb	(a) really good, e.g. *That MC was the bomb!*
	(b) cover in graffiti

bo selecta	good selection! (generally used to show you like a tune that is playing) (Popularised by the Artful Dodger/Craig David hit 'Re-Rewind The Crowd Say Bo Selecta')
bone	(a) have sex (with) (b) penis
bones	(a) dice, e.g. *Roll them bones* (b) dominoes
boo	(a) girlfriend, boyfriend (b) term of endearment, e.g. *I love you so much, boo!*
boom	good
boom-box	radio
booster	shoplifter
booty	buttocks

bootylicious	(a) sexy, often with an attractive bottom
	(b) feeling good about yourself
	(from the title of a hit song by Destiny's Child)
boo-yaa, booyaka	(a) stupendous
	(b) sound of shotgun blast
bounce	leave, move on
'bout it	genuine (short for about it), e.g. *That gold bling bling is definitely 'bout it!*
boy	friend
boyf	boyfriend
breakdancer, break-boy, break-girl	see b-boy, b-girl
brick	(a) punch, e.g. *I was bricked in a fight*
	(b) cold weather
brother	male of the same group, friend

bug	act strangely
busta	(a) weakling
	(b) telltale
	(c) spoilsport
bust this!	check this out!, have a look at this!
butt	bad, e.g. *Your rhymes are butt*

C

cabbage	money
candy bar	physically attractive female
cap	(a) bullet, e.g. *I'll pop a cap in him*
	(b) shoot
	(c) top of your head
catch the vapours	used when someone's popularity rubs off on you or you get jealous

cha	you, e.g. *I think cha is a bit out of control!*
cheddar	money
cheese	money
cherry (head)	annoying or stupid person
chickenhead	dumb person, idiot
chill	(a) mellow, laid-back
	(b) relax
chips	money
chrome	gun
chronic	marijuana
cipher	(a) event where MCs form a circle and rhyme back and forth
	(b) graffiti artist
claim	say something that may not be true, e.g. *He's claiming – I don't believe him*

clock	(a) watch, watch out
	(b) earn
	(c) hit, punch
cold	(a) mean, nasty
	(b) good
cool	(a) good, impressive
	(b) OK (usually in answer to a question)
cream	money (from 'Cash Rules Everything Around Me' by the Wu Tang Clan)
cred	credibility, e.g. *street cred*
crew	gang, clan
crib	the place someone lives
crunk	(a) get crunk: have a good time
	(b) super cool, excellent in every way
	(c) wild, e.g. *That club was really crunk*

cut	(a) haircut
	(b) track, hit (in music)
	(c) home
cuz	(a) because
	(b) cousin

D

da	the, e.g. *Play da jam*
dead presidents	US paper money, e.g. *I've got some dead presidents in my pocket!*
def	excellent (comes from US rap label Def Jam, which stands for 'definitely the best jam')
diesel	strong, manly
dig	(a) understand
	(b) like, appreciate

dime	jaw-droppingly beautiful (female) (a dime is 10 cents, suggesting 10 out of 10 on the beauty scale)
dip	leave, e.g. *Are you dipping already?*
dipped	dressed in the latest fashion
diss	insult, e.g. *Stop dissing me!* (comes from disrespect)
do	(a) hairdo (b) have sex with
dog	friend, e.g. *We're dogs*
dope	very good
down with	agreeing to do a particular activity, e.g. *I'm down with that!*
dragon	penis

drop science/ knowledge	show off your knowledge, teach, e.g. *He's dropping science with these dance moves!*
dumm	behave stupidly (from dumb)
dun	term of endearment like 'man', e.g. *How are you, dun?*

ear candy, eargasm	(something) pleasant to the ear
E.I.	Yes, let's do it, e.g. *Are you up for a fight?* – *E.I.* (stands for the first two vowels in *'yes, bring it on'*)
ends	money
eye candy	(a) (something) nice to look at (b) very pretty female

F

fade	(a) get rid of
	(b) ignore
feel	appreciate, understand
fit	attractive, good-looking
five-finger discount	theft
flava	(a) flavour
(pronounced flavour)	(b) style
flex	show how well you can do something, e.g. *a DJ flexing his skills*
floss	show off
flow	(a) money
	(b) to rhyme without stopping as in rap
fly	attractive, good-looking
fo sheezy, fa shizzle	for sure, yes
freak	(a) sexually aggressive person
	(b) have sex

freestyle	art of improvisational rapping
fresh	new, original, innovative
front	pretend to be something you're not

g'd up (pronounced jeed up)	dressed to kill
gaffle	(a) pester, harass
	(b) steal
game	(a) chat up, e.g. *Are you gaming on me?*
	(b) panache
gangsta	gangster, criminal
gasface	(a) show disrespect to
	(b) make faces at
gatt	gun

geese	be geese: leave, e.g. *I'm going to be geese*
geezer	(a) any male, e.g. *a nice geezer*
	(b) excellent
get busy	(a) eat, e.g. *I'll get busy with a few doughnuts*
	(b) have sex
ghetto fabulous	refers to a flashy style in clothes
ghost	leave
girlf	girlfriend
goolies	testicles
grill	(a) personal space, e.g. *Don't take up my grill*
	(b) face, mouth
grip	(a) money
	(b) gun
	(c) musical talent as a rapper
gum	make faces, e.g. *Please don't gum at me*

hard	tough and threatening	
hawk	wind, e.g. *The hawk is blowing*	
head	respected figure	
hella	(a) huge amount of, e.g. *That's a hella money*	
	(b) really good	
herre	here	
(pronounced her)		
highside	snub, ignore	
ho	prostitute (from whore)	
homeboy, homegirl,	(a) close friend	
homey	(b) person from the same cultural environment	
honey (dip)	attractive female	
hood	neighbourhood	
hookup	favour, good deed	
hoopin' it	playing basketball	

22

hooptie	old dilapidated car
hot	(a) physically attractive
	(b) stolen
hottie	attractive female
house	place, venue
ice	diamonds
ill	(a) act strangely, e.g. *Stop illing!*
	(b) strange
	(c) really good
in the house	here, on the premises
innit, isnit	isn't it?, aren't you? etc

J	**jacker**	carjacker
	jam	(a) track, piece of music
		(b) slam dunk (in basketball, jumping up and hitting the ball down into the basket)
		(c) any sweet food
		(d) party
	jammy	(a) penis
		(b) gun
	jenny	vagina
	jiggy	(a) get jiggy: have sex
		(b) wealthy
	jimmy	penis
	jimmy cap/hat	condom
	jone	provoke, make fun of

	jones	love interest, e.g. *my new jones*
	juice	(a) respect
		(b) alcohol
K	**keeping it real**	staying true to the roots of something
	kicks	shoes, trainers
	knob	(a) penis
		(b) idiot
	knocka	pest, nasty person
L	**lairy**	cheeky, misbehaving
	lamp	(a) hang out somewhere (like a streetlamp)
		(b) relax while other people are panicking
	lime	gathering of friends and/or family
	live	great, e.g. *This jam is really live!*

locks	dreadlocks	
luka	money	
lunch	act awkwardly	

M

mack	(a) ladies man
	(b) pimp
	(c) steal
madhatter	drug dealer
marinate	relax, hang out, e.g. *I'm marinating with my friends*
massive	large gang
max	have a lot of fun
menstral	angry

minging
(rhymes with singing)
mojo

my bad

(a) very bad
(b) very smelly
(a) magic spell or charm
(b) art of casting spells
(c) penis
used for saying *'sorry, my fault'*

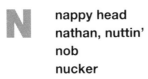

nappy head
nathan, nuttin'
nob
nucker

head with dreadlocks
nothing
have sex
(a) best friend
(b) stupid person

O

off the hook/heezy	great, wild, e.g. *The party was off the hook*
old skool	the early days of hip hop
on swo, on swoll	really big, getting bigger, e.g. *His ego is on swo*
one love!, one!	goodbye!, peace! (a greeting)

P

papes, papers	paper money
peep this!	look at this!, check this out!
peeps	people (often friends and/or family)
pen	jail, penitentiary
pep	beat up
phat	(a) cool, well done or made
	(b) PHysically ATtractive
phat pocket	(a) wealthy individual
	(b) plenty of money

piece	masterpiece (usually refers to graffiti)
play	(a) action, e.g. *Let's see some play*
	(b) go along with, agree with
playa	respected person, i.e. in the game of life
playa hater	jealous person who doesn't like to see others better themselves
played out	old, had its time, e.g. *My guitar is played out*
play yourself	make a fool of yourself
poet	rapper
pootie-tang	sex
posse	group of friends, gang
primo	friend
props	respect
pump	play music loud
punani, punany	vagina

R		
rank	mean, nasty	
rave	behave in a socially unacceptable way, often violently	
ride	car, e.g. *I'm cruising in my ride*	
rip	(a) steal	
	(b) do something well, e.g. *ripping it on the mic*	
road dog	good friend	
rock	(a) wear	
	(b) successfully entertain, e.g. *He rocked da house*	
	(c) diamond	
roll	(a) travel	
	(b) laugh	
roll on	have a good time	

s

scope	look down, for example someone's cleavage, e.g. *He was scoping her*
scrap a lick	put up a fight
scratch	money
scratching	rhythmic sound made by sliding the needle back and forth on a vinyl record (this musical effect is performed on turntables, known as '*1 and 2s*' or '*wheels of steel*', by hip hop DJs)
scrilla	money
scrubs	men with no sense of responsibility
sherm	drug-influenced, e.g. *a sherm hallucination*
short	vehicle, e.g. *riding in a short*
shorty	attractive person
shout out	congratulate

skank	(a) lewd female
	(b) horrible
slamming	(a) extremely attractive
	(b) fantastic
smell	understand, e.g. *Ya smell me?*
snow	cocaine
spliff	marijuana cigarette
step off!	go away!
step to	confront
storyteller	rapper
strapped (in)	armed
stupid	intelligent
Swayze	out of here, leaving, e.g. *I'm Swayze!*
(pronounced sway-zee)	(from the Patrick Swayze film 'Ghost')
sweat	(a) harass
	(b) flattering comments

T

tag	a graffiti artist's trademark
tax	steal, rob
thang	thing, way of doing something, e.g. *Do your thang!*
ting	thing
trackies	tracksuit bottoms
trill	rough streetwise individual
trip	overreact
twisted	(a) on drugs
	(b) drunk
	(c) wrong

U

up on it	aware
upstairs	heaven

V   **vest, jimmy vest**   condom

W

wack	bad
warrior	penis
wet	kill, shoot
wicked	good
wordsmith	rapper
word up	yes, I agree
wreck	(a) accomplish, perform well
	(b) destroy completely

Y **yo**

(a) you
(b) your
(c) hey (used to get attention)
(d) yes

Z **zooted**

on drugs

OTHER TITLES AVAILABLE

Language Glossaries

American English/English American
Australian English/English Australian
Irish English/English Irish
Geordie English
Lancashire English
Rhyming Cockney Slang
Scouse English
Yiddish English/English Yiddish
Scottish English/English Scottish
Yorkshire English
A Queer Companion
(A rough guide to gay slang)
Ultimate Language of Flowers
Hip Hop English
Rude Rhyming Slang

The Death of Kings (A medical history
of the Kings & Queens of England)

Literary Quiz & Puzzle Books

Jane Austen
Brontë Sisters
Charles Dickens
Gilbert & Sullivan
Thomas Hardy
Sherlock Holmes
Shakespeare

All of these titles are available from good
booksellers or by contacting the publisher:

Abson Books London
5 Sidney Square London E1 2EY
Tel 020 7790 4737 Fax 020 7790 7346
email absonbooks@aol.com